A Little Golden Book® Biography

By Trin Betrell • Illustrated by Manu Cunhas

Golden Books
An imprint of Random House Children's Books
A division of Penguin Random House LLC
1745 Broadway, New York, NY 10019
penguinrandomhouse.com
rhcbooks.com

Library of Congress Control Number: 2024952544
ISBN 979-8-217-02553-4 (trade) — ISBN 979-8-217-02554-1 (ebook)
Manufactured in the United States of America
10 9 8 7 6 5 4 3 2 1
The authorized representative in the EU for product safety and compliance is
Penguin Random House Ireland, Morrison Chambers, 32 Nassau Street,
Dublin D02 YH68, Ireland. https://eu-contact.penguin.ie

Pink is one of the greatest pop musicians of all time. She dazzles crowds with her amazing live performances, raspy voice, and songs with bold, honest lyrics. She can even sing while flying through the air!

Pink was born Alecia Beth Moore on September 8, 1979, in Doylestown, Pennsylvania. She grew up with her mother, father, and older brother, Jason. Her friends nicknamed her Pink when she was young. Later, she used it as her stage name.

Pink took gymnastics lessons for many years, starting when she was four. She worked hard at it, practicing five days a week and competing in tournaments. She dreamed of one day going to the Olympics.

But Pink's real love was music. She was inspired by her dad, who played guitar and wrote songs. She knew from a young age that she wanted to be a singer.

Even though she had asthma, a health condition that can make it difficult to breathe, Pink had a powerful voice. She took singing lessons and sang in a gospel choir at church.

While growing up, Pink went through some hard times at home. Her mom and dad argued a lot, and when she was ten years old, they divorced.

Pink became involved in all kinds of activities to help ease her sadness and stay busy. She played soccer, took up skateboarding, and wrote poetry about her feelings. Soon, she was turning her poems into songs and writing music.

In high school, Pink wrote more songs as the lead singer in a band called Middleground. After the band broke up, she started performing in music clubs around Philadelphia. She danced and sang backup for a hip-hop group called Schoolz of Thought.

When she was fourteen, a DJ at a popular nightclub gave her a chance to sing onstage by herself. She belted out a song by the R & B artist Mary J. Blige. The crowd loved it!

After that, Pink sang at the club every week. One night, a talent agent from a big record company was in the audience. He offered Pink the chance to try out for an all-girl R & B band called Basic Instinct. She got the job! Unfortunately, the group broke up before they released any music.

Soon, Pink joined another group called Choice. She sang with her two other bandmates for three years before pursuing a career as a solo artist.

Pink's first solo album, *Can't Take Me Home*, came out in 2000. Pink didn't just sing on the record. She cowrote seven of the songs, too. The dance-pop and R & B album was very popular, and the song "There You Go" became her first hit. Pink was finally a star!

After the success of *Can't Take Me Home*, Pink wanted to take a break from R & B music and try something else. She worked on her next album with one of her childhood idols, Linda Perry from the popular rock group 4 Non Blondes. Pink and Linda had different musical styles, but they made an excellent team.

When the pop-rock album *Missundaztood* came out in 2001, Pink's fans loved the new sound. It sold over 13 million copies. The biggest song on the album, "Get the Party Started," flew to the top of the charts!

Pink always puts on a thrilling show for her fans. There are awesome dance routines, colorful fireworks, and amazing aerial stunts.

Using the gymnastics skills she learned as a kid and training with some of the best aerialist coaches, she flips, spins, and soars above the crowd attached to bungee cords. Pink says she sings best when upside down!

Whether she's upside down or right side up, Pink connects with her audience through her music. She writes songs about things that are meaningful to her, like love, family, the state of the world, and the importance of being true to yourself.

Pink's albums have sold millions of copies. And even though Pink is known for her rock-influenced pop, you can find other musical styles in her work, including dance, punk, hip-hop, folk, soul, and New Wave.

In 2005, Pink proposed to her boyfriend, Carey Hart, a professional motocross racer. During one of his competitions, she held up a sign that read, "Will you marry me?" After he drove past her, she added the word "Serious!" When Carey saw that, he pulled over in the middle of the race to say yes! The next year, they got married.

Pink and Carey have two children, Willow and Jameson. Being a rock star and a mom isn't always easy, but Pink makes it work. She even brings her kids with her on tour. Of all the things she has accomplished, Pink says being a mom is "the most incredible thing I've ever done."

Pink has collaborated with many famous musicians, like Kenny Chesney, Sia, and Eminem. But she enjoys making music with her own family best. She and her dad sang a song he wrote while serving in the Vietnam War called "I Have Seen the Rain." And she released a duet with her daughter called "Cover Me in Sunshine." Willow even performs with her mom during some of her shows!

As an activist, Pink fights for causes she believes in. She speaks out against bullying and supports charities that help animals and kids, including Save the Children and People for the Ethical Treatment of Animals (PETA).

At the 2019 E! People's Choice Awards, Pink was honored for everything she has done to help others. "One person can make a difference," she told fans as she accepted the People's Champion award. "Get involved. . . . Get together with your friends and change the world."

Pink is a Grammy Award–winning musician who has used her voice, courage, creativity, and athleticism to become pop royalty. She inspires others through her music and activism—and by never being afraid to be herself or speak her truth.

Fly high, Pink!